INTRODUCTION

This book is a communicative speaking course designed for students who are leaning English as a foreign language (EFL) or those who are learning English as a second language (ESL). The course is speaking based, with strong communicative flavour, in other words the book is based on Communicative Language Teaching (CLT) approach. This book aims at developing the speaking skills among (EFL&ESL) students. It is based on the philosophy Communicative Language Teaching (CLT).

The course has been designed to help teachers to vary their teaching techniques and activities to meet all individual differences among students who are in need to make learning fun. This book has been taught through a variety of communicative learner's centred *activities* which have been selected and graded to be (as much as possible) suitable for the students' interests, preferences, needs, age, abilities...., etc. These activities have been assumed to be interactive interesting, motivating, and secured. The materials have been assumed to be authentic.

Table of Contents. **PAGE**

• The main objectives of the book

This book aims at helping students develop the following speaking skills:

1- Introducing the ideas in a logical order.

2- Inviting someone for a visit.

3- Giving directions.

4- Giving positive and negative commands.

5- Making comparisons.

6- Describing (people- objects-dreams- pictures-places).

7- Asking for and telling about the time.

8- Speaking fluently and naturally

9- Speaking without remarkable pauses or hesitation, repetition or redundancy.

10- Stopping when the meaning is completed (turn-taking).

11-Using various appropriate strategic devices to enhance the clarity of the meaning such as (fillers, pauses, ellipses, etc....).

12 -Producing English sounds correctly.

13-Differentiating between consonant sounds correctly (/t∫/, /∫/& /f/, /v/ & /p/, /b/ & /s/, /z/ & /ð/, /θ/)

14- Differentiating between vowel sounds correctly (/i:/, /i -/ɔ/ /:ɔ)

15- Pronouncing words with intelligible stress.

16- Producing intelligible intonation (raising /falling) to express different meanings.

17- Selecting the appropriate vocabulary to express the main idea.

18- Using vocabulary in different context.

19- Using abstract and concrete vocabulary in sentences correctly.

20-Using appropriate body language such as: gestures, facial expressions, eye contact, and hands along with verbal language. in order to convey the meaning.

21-Using grammar structure correctly.

22. Forming questions and answers correctly.

23-Choosing the most appropriate tense (past simple, present simple and future simple)

- **Content of the book:**

The goal of the book is to develop speaking skills among the (EFL&ESL) students. So the book consists of six units including five lessons for each one and each lesson involves two activities. Each unit will last for five periods, 45 minutes each. Therefore, the content of the book is seriously selected so as to reach this particular goal as follows.

Unit 1 (New Classes)

Lesson 1: Giving directions

Lesson 2: Listen and do

Lesson 3: My dreams

Lesson 4: My first day at my school

Lesson 5: How to pronounce" instruction"?

Unit 2 (Family, home and work)

Lesson 1: My family

Lesson 2: Jobs

Lesson 3: What job do you like to have?

Lesson 4: A doctor's day

Lesson 5: A, B, C order

Unit 3 (How tall are you?)

Lesson 1: He is the tallest?

Lesson 2: Numbers, Numbers

Lesson 3: The plane is the fastest vehicle

Lesson 4: What do you know about Egypt?

Lesson 5: What do these words mean?

Unit 4 (Things we can do)

Lesson 1: I can walk, I can talk

Lesson 2: How long can camels live?

Lesson 3: Helen Keller

Lesson 4: Life in the future

Lesson 5: Say English vowels

Unit 5 (Time to see Egypt)

Lesson 1: Time table

Lesson 2: What time will you have lunch?

Lesson 3: Our holiday

Lesson 4: E-mail me

Lesson 5: Don't be puzzled

Unit 6 (Soha's poem)

Lesson 1: Internet magazine

Lesson 2: What were they doing?

Lesson 3: A helicopter was flying in the sky

Lesson 4: Retell a story?

Lesson 5: Say English consonants

- **Techniques and Activities Used in the Light of (CLT)Approach**:-

Actually, CLT approach presents an organizational framework on which English teachers can use. The main teaching activities and techniques included in this study are:

- *Brainstorming Role-playing*
- *Dialogues*
- *Puzzles*
- *Games*
- *Interviews*
- *Information Gap*
- *Jigsaw*
- *Discussions-Debates Problem solving*
- *Songs*

- **Teaching Aids:**

pictures –audio- videos - word cards –flash cards – real objects – maps- diagrams -CD player-tables-graphics- coloured markers.

- **Guidelines for teachers for implementing a multi-activities in teaching speaking (EFL&ESL) students students:**

1. Vary your teaching techniques to meet all individual differences among students.

2. Start your lesson by warming up students to prepare them to receive the lesson.

3. Encourage your students to pair-up and co-operate with each other in groups to practice different activities.

4. Help your students gain self-esteem by giving them the opportunity to demonstrate mastery level of their performance while expressing themselves.

5. Encourage your students to participate in competitive activities and observe them while they are involved in these activities.

6. Encourage your students by using supporting words or gestures of satisfaction such as : "good, excellent, go on, yes, alright...etc."

8- Develop a friendly classroom atmosphere so as to promote students spontaneous use of oral language.

9- Provide your students with help when necessary.

10- Use formative evaluation techniques.

11- Emphasis on learning to communicate through interaction in the target language.

12- Enhance of the learner's own personal experiences as important contributing elements to classroom activities.

13- Attempt to link classroom language learning with language activities outside the classroom.

14- Provide opportunities for learners to experiment and try out what they know.

15-Be tolerant of learners' errors as they indicate that the learners are building up their communicative competence.

16- Provide opportunities for learners to develop both accuracy and fluency.

17-Link the different skills such as speaking, reading, and listening together, since they usually occur so in the real world.

18-Let students induce or discover grammar rules.

Unit one

New classes

Aims of the unit

This unit aims at helping you to:

- Give and respond to directions.

- Give and respond to commands.

- Ask for help in the classroom.

- Perform a short dialogue.

- Describe and ask about dreams.

- Report past events.

Lesson One

Giving directions

- **_Objectives:_ -**

  By the end of the lesson, you are expected to:

- _Give and respond to directions._

- _Give and respond to commands._

- **_Activity type:_** _Pair- work /group work_

- **_Time needed:_** _45 minutes_

Activity One

"Where am I?"

Activity Two

"A blindfolded classmate"

Fold your eyes and listen to your friends to reach the target:-

- Turn right

- Turn left

- Go straight on

- Stop!

- It's on your left

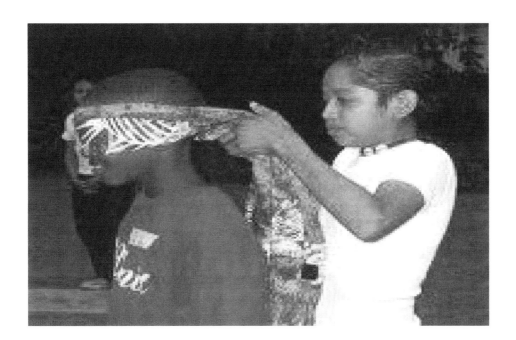

- *Objectives:* -

  By the end of the lesson, you are expected to:

- **Say instructions in sequence and carry them out.**

- **Give positive and negative commands**

- *Activity type:* **Pair- work /Individual work**

- *Time needed:* **45 minutes**

Activity One

Aerobics class

Stand up in rows, like in an aerobics class, and then follow the instructions:

- Look to the left

- Look to the right

- Look out the window

- Raise your left hand

- Raise your right hand

- Put your fingers in your ears

- Close your eyes

- Turn your head to the left

Activity Two

Captain Maged says...

- *<u>Stand in a big circle, and listen to the leader who gives commands, when only you listen to "Captain Maged says" you must follow the order.</u>*

- *Captain Maged says, "Close your eyes."*

- *Captain Maged says, "Put your fingers in your ears."*

- *Captain Maged says, "Hold your nose."*

- *Captain Maged says, "Turn your head to the right"*

- *Captain Maged says," Jump up on your feet for two minutes"*

Lesson Three

My dreams

- ***Objectives: -***

    By the end of the lesson, you are expected to:

- *Talk about dreams.*

- *Use the present continuous tense to describe current actions.*

- Forming questions and answers correctly. (Using the present continuous tense)

- ***Activity type:*** *Pair- work /group work*

- ***Time needed:*** *45 minutes*

Activity One

Charades

Act out the action in the picture. As your team guess the action, they should form a complete sentence in the present continuous tense.

- You are fishing
- You are riding bikes
- You are laughing
- You are sleeping and dreaming

Activity Two

What is in your dream?

Close your eyes and try to remember one of your dreams you can take notes. Write down at least one such dream. Then, stand up and walk around and get another classmate, to tell you his dream, and discuss it with your teacher.

My dream

....

....

....

....

My friend's dream

....

....

....

....

Lesson Four

The first day at my school

- ***Objectives: -***

  By the end of the lesson, you are expected to:

  - *Perform a dialogue about a day at school.*

  - *Ask and answer questions about past events.*

  - *Use various appropriate strategic devices to enhance the clarity of the meaning such as (fillers, pauses, ellipses)*

  - *Use appropriate body language such as: gestures, facial expressions, eye contact, and hands along with language in order to convey the meaning.*

- ***Activity type:*** *Pair- work /group-work*

- ***Time needed:*** *45 minutes*

Activity One

Try to guess what happened

- ***Stand in two rows (face to face) in two rows, the first row declares real problems that they faced before the other students try to guess the reasons.***

Ahmed: My watch was stopped working.

Kamal: you dropped into the food while cooking.

Rami: My pencil was broken

Karim: You tried to open your desk with it.

Sami: My book was damaged.

Nour: your cut some pages, etc.

Activity two

Lost Voices

Convey the situation on the paper to the class without speaking as you have lost your voice.

- I'm sorry, I came late because I overslept and missed the bus.
- I think I got lost, how can I go to Ramses station, please?
- I finished my homework but I couldn't sleep afterwards.
- We had a party yesterday, but I didn't eat cake, my brother was hungry and he ate the whole cake.

Lesson Five
How to pronounce instruction?

- ***Objectives: -***

  By the end of the lesson, you are expected to:
- *Produce intelligible stress.*
- *Ask and answer questions about past events.*
- *Produce intelligible intonation (raising /falling) to express different meanings.*
- ***Activity type:*** *groupwork*
- ***Time needed:*** *45 minutes*

Activity One

Song: First Day of School

- **Listen to the following song about the first day at school. Express your point of view and then try to compose your own song. After singing with your teacher, you can participate your partner.**

First Day of School

Good morning, how are you?

This is the very first day of school.

I'm so glad to meet you,

others will be too,

just come in the classroom,

there's lots of things to do.

Original Author Unknown

Activity Two
Say Instruction

- *Underline the stressed syllable of each individual word and then (in groups). Put them in meaningful sentences. In pairs ask questions about these sentences.*

(Shouting – exciting – pronunciation – helpful – funny – useful – expensive- bag – then – after – finally – next).

Unit Two

Family, home and work

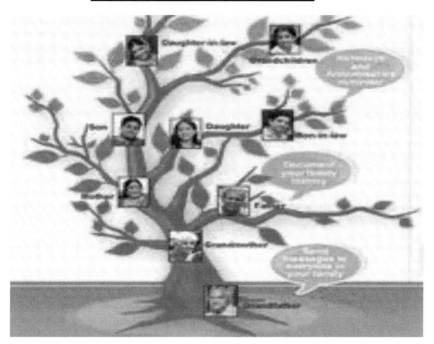

General aims :

This unit aims at helping you to:

- Describe family relationships.
- Give personal information.
- Say what people are called.
- Describe and ask about working life.
- Describe different jobs.
- Ask and answer about personal preferences.
- Describe doctor's routine in detail.
- Make sentences from prompts.

Lesson One

He is the tallest?

- ***Objectives: -***

    By the end of the lesson, you are expected to:

- *Describe family relationships.*

- *Give personal information.*

- *Say what people are called.*

- ***Activity type:*** *Pair- work /group-work*

- ***Time needed:*** *45 minutes*

Activity One

What about your family?

▪*Stand up to introduce your partner to the class in not more than two minutes.*

- *My friend is Ahmed.*
- *He's 12 years old.*
- *He was born in Cairo.*
- *His father is a doctor.*
- *He has three brothers and one sister.*
- *His uncle Nabil is still single.*

Activity Two
Ball Game

Stand up in a circle around your teacher. A ball is tossed to you and the teacher asks a question, "One of the following". You then respond and throw the ball back to your teacher.

Teacher	Student
What is your name?	
How old are you?	
What is your grandfather's name?	
What is your grandmother called?	
Is your uncle single or married?	
(If married) How many sons has your uncle got?	
How many daughters has your uncle got?	
Who is your dad's brother?	

Jobs

- *Objectives: -*

    By the end of the lesson, you are expected to:

  - *Describe and ask about working life.*

  - *Describe different jobs.*

- *Activity type:* *Pair- work /group-work*

- *Time needed:* *45 minutes*

Activity One

Role playing

▪ *You (Hesham) and your friend (Wael) were at the club yesterday, you met a new friend. Introduce (Nabil) to your friend.*

Hesham: "Hello, I'm Hesham. I'm a businessman.

Nabil: How do you do Hesham, my name is Nabil. I'm a doctor.

Hesham: Nice to meet you Dr. Nabil, where do you work?

Nabil: I work in a big hospital. and you?

Hesham: I work in a tourist company.

Nabil: Great! Where do you live?

Hesham: I live in Giza.

Nabil: It is a great place; I live in Nasr City.

Hesham: I think we are going to be friends.

Nabil: Could you give me your mobile number and e-mail address.

Hesham: With pleasure.

Wael: Hello Hesham, hello Mr Ahh................

Hesham: Hello Wael, this is my new friend Dr. Nabil.

Wael: Hello Dr. Nabil. Nice to meet you.

Hesham: Doctor Nabil lives in Nasr City and works in a big hospital.

Wael: Great! I'm an English teacher, I work in a language school, and I live in London too.

Activity Two
Solve this problem

Stand in two lines. Line A has cards with problems written on them. You should tell your problem to the student facing you. Line B is then should offer advice for the problem.

A: My car is not working   B: You should go to the mechanic.

A: I cannot understand this exercise   B: You can ask your teacher.

A: I want to eat fresh bread   B: You can go to the bakery.

A: I want to buy a new T-shirt   B: you can go to the clothes shop

Lesson Three

What job do you like to have?

- *Objectives:* -

  By the end of the lesson, you are expected to:

  - *Describe different jobs.*

  - *Ask and answer about personal preferences.*

  - *Speaking without remarkable pauses or hesitation, repetition or redundancy.*

- *Activity type: group-work*

- *Time needed: 45 minutes*

Activity One

Can You Guess Who I Am?

- *Start asking your friend questions to find out who is being impersonated. Only yes/no answers may be given*

  - Do you live in Egypt?

  - Do you have a family?

  - Do you have children?

  - Do you work at the university?

  - Do you work in a company?

  - Do you like chemistry?

  - Do you invent something?

  - Are you fat?

  - Are you tall?

  - Do you live in America now?

  - Are you Dr. Ahmed Zewail?

Activity Two

Jigsaw

- *Listen to your teacher while he names a job, as below, and the first team must try to say a relating word, while the second team have to put it in a complete sentence.*

Teacher	Group B	Group A
A doctor	hospital	A doctor works in a hospital.
A teacher	White board	A teacher writes on a white board.
A policeman	thief	A policeman must catch thieves.
A carpenter	chairs	A carpenter makes chairs.
secretary	office	A secretary works in an office.
A baker	bakery	A baker works in a bakery.

Teacher	Group A	Group B
Nurse		
Postman		
Mechanic		
Engineer		
Farmer		
Tourist guide		

Lesson Four

A doctor's day

- ***Objectives: -***

  By the end of the lesson, you are expected to:

  - *Describe doctor's routine in detail.*

  - *Using various appropriate strategic devices to enhance the clarity of the meaning such as (pauses, ellipses, etc....).*

- ***Activity type:*** *group-work*

- ***Time needed:*** *45 minutes*

Activity One

If you were a doctor for a day, how could you help people?

Stand up in a circle and each one should write down three suggestions to the above question. Then, go around the circle and ask everyone for a suggestion. Nobody will be allowed to repeat an idea that has already been given before.

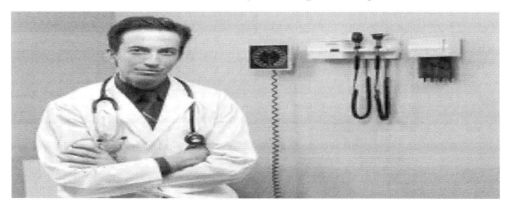

<u>Students' suggestions:</u>

1- I could examine patients.
2-..
3-..
4-..

Activity Two

The doctor and the patient

- *Listen to the interview between Ahmed (a patient) and Dr. Khalid, and then set up a similar dialogue in pairs.*

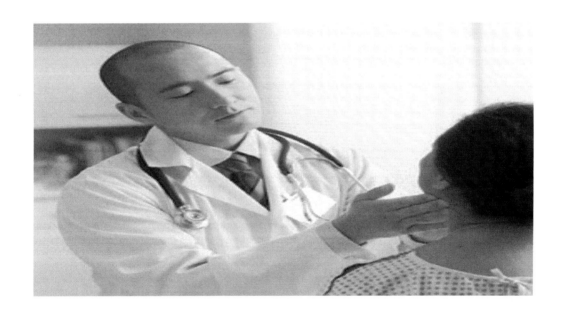

AHMED: Good morning, Dr. Khalid!

DR. KHALID: Good morning! What's wrong with you?

AHMED: I have fever since yesterday.

DR. KHALID: Have you any other problem?

AHMED: I also feel headache.

DR. KHALID: Let me check your fever……… Don't worry, there is nothing serious. I am giving you the medicine, and you will be all right in a few days.

AHMED: Thank you, doctor.

DR. KHALID: I shall recommend at least two days rest for you.

AHMED: Thank you very much. Please tell me how shall I take this medicine?

DR. KHALID: This medicine is for one day only. Take this dose as soon as you reach your home and the second at 3 pm and the third at night before sleeping.

AHMED: What should I eat doctor?

DR. KHALID: You should eat only light food. You can take milk and fresh fruit also.

AHMED: How much shall I pay you doctor?

DR. KHALID: one hundred only.

AHMED: Here it is please. Thanks doctor.

DR. KHALID: It's all right.

AHMED: Thank you doctor.

Lesson Five

A, B, C order

- *Objectives: -*

   By the end of the lesson, you are expected to:

- *Practice ordering words alphabetically.*

- *practice and differentiate between sounds/th/-(this) &/th/ (thing)*

- *Use various appropriate strategic devices to enhance the clarity of the meaning such as (pauses, ellipses, etc....).*

   - *Activity type: group-work*

   - *Time needed: 45 minutes*

Activity One

Play this game

- *Stand in lines. Then the teacher draws with his finger an imaginary letter of the alphabet on the back of the students at the end of the lines. They must do the same with the student in front of them and so on. The students with the marker are supposed to run to the board and write any word that begins with that letter. The other student has to put it in a meaningful sentence.*

Activity two:

Think and say

- *Listen, say, and discuss the difference between the /th/ð/ sound and /th /θ /sound, add words with the same sound.*

/th/	/th/
this	thin
father	both
-----	-----
-----	-----
-----	-----
-----	-----

Unit Three

How tall are you?

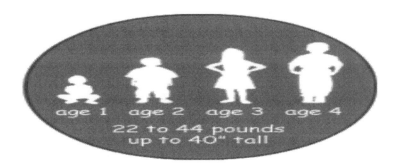

Aims of the unit:

This unit aims at helping students to:

- Compare and describe people.

- Ask and answer questions about weight, age, and height.

- Express quantities.

- Recognize and say numbers up to one million.

- Use comparative and superlative adjectives.

- Describe and compare vehicles' age, size, height, and speed.

- Describe and compare places.

- Ask for and give measurements, age and dimension of places.

Lesson One

He is the tallest?

- ***Objectives: -***

  By the end of the lesson, you are expected to:

  - *Compare and describe people.*

  - *Ask and answer questions about weight, age, and height.*

- ***Activity type:*** *group-work*

- ***Time needed:*** *45 minutes*

Activity One

Ball throw

Stand up in the circle to throw the ball to your friend and ask him a question. The student then responds and throws the ball back to another friend.

How tall are you?	I'm one meter and 50 cm tall.
How much do you weigh?	**I weigh 45 kg.**
...................................?	....

Measuring height & weight (child)

Measuring height & weight (man)

Measuring chest & waist (man)   Measuring bust, waist, and hip (woman)

Measuring height & weight (woman)   Measuring height & weight (baby)

Activity Two

"Complete my information"

Fill in the blanks by asking each other appropriate questions.

Table one:

Name	Nabila	Rami	Ahmed
Age:	60		35
Height:	155		177
Weight:	67		73

Table Two:

Name	Nabila	Rami	Ahmed
Age:		10	
Height:		93	
Weigh:		31	

Lesson Two
Numbers, Number

- **_Objectives: -_**

    By the end of the lesson, you are expected to:

    - _Express quantities._

    - _Recognize and say numbers up to one million._

- **_Activity type:_** _group-work_

- **_Time needed:_** _45 minutes_

Activity One
Secret Number

- **_Think of a secret number and write it on the paper. The other students take turns guessing what the number is._**

Activity Two

The Numbers Game

• Everybody must think up a set of numbers that have a special meaning, and the other students have to guess what the meaning is by asking questions and suggesting answers.

12-8-1999

How old are you?

Is this your birthday?

Is it the birthday of a family member?

8787

Do you have a car?

Does your father have a car?

Are these numbers of your car?

1,000,000

Is this a personal number for you? Yes?

Is it a password number?

Is it your secret pin number?

Lesson Three

Is the plane the fastest vehicle?

- **Objectives: -**

   By the end of the lesson, you are expected to:

   - Use comparative and superlative adjectives.

   - Describe and compare vehicles' age, size, height, and speed.

- **Activity type:** group-work

- **Time needed:** 45 minutes

Activity One

Jigsaw

Listen and complete the diagram then compare the three versions with your partner.

	Car	Ship	Plane
Age	50	40	100
Height			
Weight			
Length			
Speed			

For example;

- The car is older than the ship.

- The plane is the oldest.

Activity Two

Acting with Comparatives and Superlatives

Comparatives and Superlatives

• *Each group is given a word to act out as comparative/superlative and the rest of the class must figure out what word they are showing and put it in a sentence.*

big bigger biggest

funny, funnier, funniest;

small, smaller, smallest;

smart, smarter, smartest;

happy, happier, happiest;

Lesson Four

What do you know about Egypt?

- **_Objectives: -_**

  By the end of the lesson, you are expected to:

  - _Describe and compare places._

  - _Ask for and give measurements, age and dimension of places._

  - _Speak without remarkable pauses or hesitation, repetition or redundancy_

- **_Activity type:_** _group-work_

- **_Time needed:_** _45 minutes_

Activity one:
Measure and ask

- _Each pair chooses one object. The first student measures the length, the height and the width of the chosen object in the classroom then records the measurements in a piece of paper and attaches it with glue on the object he has measured after that the other student asks him some questions about the length, the height and the width._

Activity Two:-

"What do you know about Egypt?"

Look at the following pictures and discuss what you know about Egypt, listen carefully to the CD player and take notes and then set up a dialogue in pairs

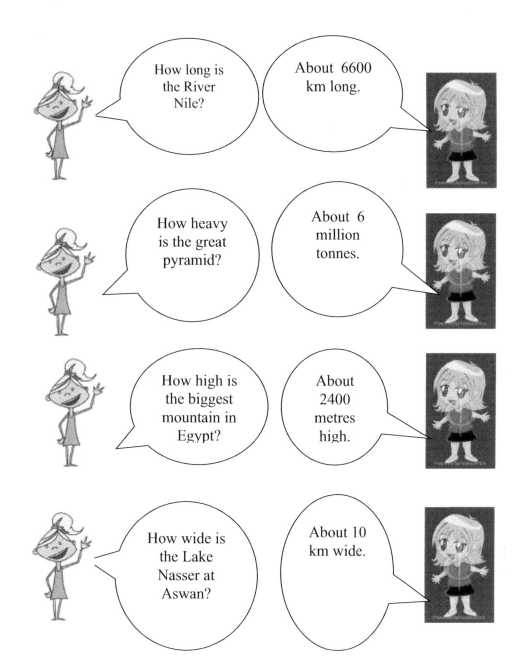

How long is the River Nile?

About 6600 km long.

How heavy is the great pyramid?

About 6 million tonnes.

How high is the biggest mountain in Egypt?

About 2400 metres high.

How wide is the Lake Nasser at Aswan?

About 10 km wide.

Lesson Five
What do these words mean?

- *Objectives: -*

  By the end of the lesson, you are expected to:

- *Say sentences using the present simple tense.*
- *Speak fluently and naturally.*
- *Speak without remarkable pauses or hesitation, repetition or redundancy.*
- *Differentiate between consonant sounds correctly (/tʃ/, /ʃ/& /f/, /v/ & /p/, /b/ & /s/, /z/ & /ð/, /θ/)*
- *Activity type: group-work*
- *Time needed: 45 minutes*

Activity one:
Spin a Sentence -

Form a circle. One player "leader" stands in the centre of the circle. He calls out a single word that contains a certain consonant (/tʃ/, /ʃ/& /f/, /v/ & /p/, /b/ & /s/, /z/ & /ð/, /θ/) followed by a number (3, 4, 5 or 6). The leader then closes his eyes, spins around in the circle once or twice and then points to the student he/she is now facing. That player must now say a sentence using the number of words the leader has given, including the leader's word.

Very-5	*- It is very hot today.*
Without-5	*-The tea is without sugar,"*
Five- 4	*-I have five books*
Zoo -6	*-I went to the zoo yesterday*

Activity Two:

Giving examples of...

You should try to say a single word that contains a certain consonant (/tʃ/, /ʃ/& /f/, /v/ &/p/, /b/ & /s/, /z/ & /ð/, /θ/), Then the other student put this word in a meaningful sentence as in the following:

Family- father.   *Clothes -shirt*

Animal -zebra   *Sport –basketball*

Unit Four

Things we can do

Aims of the unit:

By the end of the unit students are supposed to:

- Ask for and give information about the students' abilities.

- Describe a camel.

- Express opinions and ideas with "I think".

- Describe past abilities using "could or was able."

- Use sense verbs see, taste etc.

- Speculate about the future.

- Talk about health care.

- Learn about English vowels.

Lesson One

<u>I can walk, I can talk</u>

- **<u>*Objectives:*</u>** *-*

  By the end of the lesson, you are expected to:

  - *Talk about the five main senses.*
  - *Ask and answer questions about what someone can do (Use can to express ability).*

- **<u>*Activity type:*</u>** *group-work*

- **<u>*Time needed:*</u>** *45 minutes*

Activity One

Super Bingo

List five things that you can do., then list five things that you cannot do. Walk around the room and ask the necessary questions to find students who share their abilities/experiences:

Can you swim?

Can you touch your feet 30 times?

Can you run in one place for 60 seconds?

Activity Two

It's in the Bag

Close their eyes and put one hand in the bag to choose the item and describe what you feel

- *It is round and thin. I can hear it.*
- *It is red and round, I can taste it*
- *It is made of glass; I can smell it.*
- *It is like a square I can see it.*

Lesson Two

How long can camels live?

- ***Objectives: -***

    By the end of the lesson, you are expected to:

    - *Describe a camel.*

    - *Express opinions and ideas with "I think".*

    - *Practice forming questions.*

- ***Activity type:*** *pair- work, group-work*

- ***Time needed:*** *45 minutes*

Activity One

Ask me later

- ***Make up a sentence imagining that it is an answer to a question. Each one tells his answers and others give possible questions about the life of a camel. You should write them on a paper.***

- About 15 or 16 days
- About 50 Km per Hour
- About two metres high
- Up to 40 years

Activity Two
Mix-Freeze-Pair

Walk around the classroom at random until you listen "Freeze and Pair!" Everyone stops in his place and forms pairs with the person closest to him. Now in pairs interview each other about camel's life.

1-	How long		run?
2-	How tall		carry?
3-	How far		live without water?
4-	How fast	can camels	grow?
5-	How much		live?
6-	How long		walk in one day?
7-	How many litres of water		drink?

Match and answer the above questions:-

age	Up to 2 m.
height	50 litres
walk	15-15 days
run	100 kg
carry	50 km per hour
litres of water	Up to 40 years
Live without water	50 km per day

Lesson Three

Helen Keller

- ***Objectives: -***

  By the end of the lesson, you are expected to:

  - *Describe past abilities using "could or was able"*

  - *Use sense verbs see, taste etc.*

- ***Activity type:*** *group-work*

- ***Time needed:*** *45 minutes*

Activity One

The life of Helen Keller

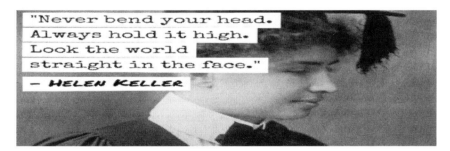

- Speak about Helen Killer, we might divide a short biography of her into stand-alone segments on: *(1) Her childhood, (2) Her family life, (3) Her teacher Anne Sullivan, (4) Braille (5) Her work for deaf and blind people.*

- One student from each group joins other students assigned to the same segment. Discuss the main points of your segment to rehearse the presentations.

Activity Two

<u>Memory game</u>

Sit together in a circle. The first one must say a phrase concerning one of the five senses, for example "I see the sea." The next student must repeat what the first student said, "He sees the sea," and add a phrase of his own such as, "I hear the bell."

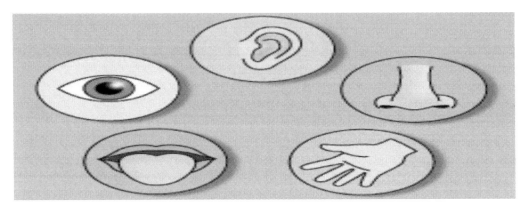

- •"Ahmed sees the sea,

- •"Karim hears the waves,"

, and

- •"I taste an ice cream."

Lesson Four

Life in the Future

- ***Objectives: -***

    By the end of the lesson, you are expected to:

    - *Speculate about the future.*

    - *Talk about health care.*

    - *Speak without remarkable pauses or hesitation, repetition or redundancy.*

- ***Activity type:*** *group-work*

- ***Time needed:*** *45 minutes*

Activity One

Will mimes

Look in a crystal ball and then mime what they see. Work in pairs one student miming the problem and the other suggests the solution.

My bag is heavy	” Stop. I'll carry it for you.”
My friend is crying	“I know. I'll give him my ice-cream.”
My leg is broken	"Don't worry I will call a doctor."

Activity Two

For or Against

- *Sit around the table face to face to mention your points of view-the first group support the idea but the second group stands against it. think about it and make notes. When you are ready start. Will we be able to have a better life in the future? Cover the following points*

(Doctors- hospitals - medicine -food)

For	Against

Lesson Five

Say English Vowels

Short&Long vowel sounds

- **Objectives: -**

    By the end of the lesson, you are expected to:

    ▪ *Differentiate between vowel sounds /i/ & /i/*

    ▪ *Produce short sounds correctly.*

    ▪ *Use vocabulary in different context.*

- **Activity type:** *pair-work & whole class-work*

- **Time needed:** *45 minutes*

Activity One

Vowel sounds

- ***Write it the following two columns the appropriate words with the identical sounds /i: / or /i/ using different marker. Then ask and answer questions using the selected words:***

E.g.

    A: Do you speak English?

    B: Yes, I do.

    A: Was the film interesting?

    B: Yes, it was.

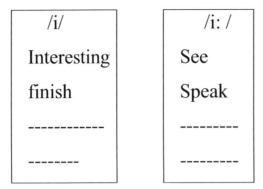

/i/	/i: /
Interesting	See
finish	Speak
-----------	---------
--------	---------

Activity Two

("Farmer in the Dell")

●*Sing the following song in chorale with your teacher and try to create a similar one*

("Farmer in the Dell")

The short (a) is lamb, the short a is in lamb - /a/ /a/ /a/ /a/ /a/ /a/, the short a is in lamb.

The short e is in hen, the short e is in hen - /e/ /e/ /e/ /e/ /e/ /e/, the short e is in hen.

The short i is in pig, the short i is in pig - /i/ /i/ /i/ /i/ /i/ /i/, the short i is in pig.

The short o is in fox, the short o is in fox - /o/ /o/ /o/ /o/ /o/ /o/, the short o is in fox.

The short u is in bug, the short u is in bug - /u/ /u/ /u/ /u/ /u/ /u/, the short u is in bug.

Unit Five
Time to see Egypt

Aims of the unit:

By the end of the unit, you are supposed to:

- Ask and answer about time and time table of the future events.

- Use "will" to express future events

- Use analogue watch to express the timetable.

- Ask and tell someone about time.

- Describe famous places in Egypt with adjectives.

- Describe a holiday.

- Invite someone for a visit.

- Express plans in the future using "will".

- Practise simultaneous words (words which have the same pronunciation but different meanings.

Lesson One

Our Time table

- ***Objectives: -***

  By the end of the lesson, you are expected to:

  - *Ask and answer about time and time table of the future events.*

  - *Use "will" to express future events.*

- ***Activity type: group-work***

- ***Time needed: 45 minutes***

Activity One

Stop and Talk -

- ***Listen to the CD and record the timetable for a journey next week. Then ask the student faces you one question and the other student has to answer it.***

1-What time do we leave Cairo next week?	7:30
2-What time do we arrive at the hotel?	11:15
3-What time will we have our lunch?	2:00
4-What time will we start the camel ride?	3:00
5-What time will we go for a boat trip?	4:15
6-What time will we eat dinner at the Bedouin village?	8:30

Activity Two
<u>A reasonable plan</u>

• *Negotiate with your group about the appropriate sequencing to you. using pictures for alternative satisfactory sequences for the next week plan:*

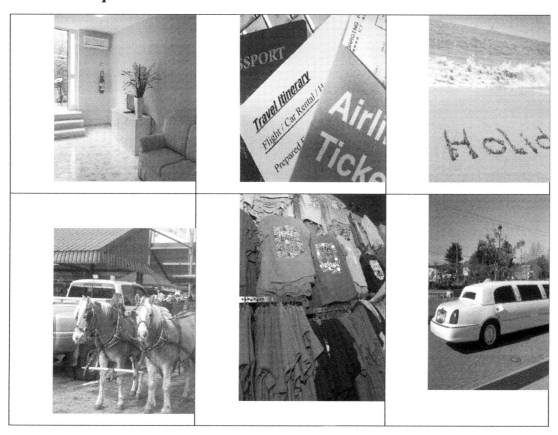

Lesson Two

What time will you have lunch?

- *Objectives: -*

  By the end of the lesson, you are expected to:

- *Produce intelligible intonation (raising /falling) to express different meanings.*

- *Differentiate between consonant sounds correctly.*

- *Ask and tell someone about time.*

- *Activity type: group-work*
- *Time needed: 45 minutes*

Activity One

Hip-Hop Around the Clock

Stand in a circle with moveable clocks evenly placed around the circle. Dance around the circle. When the music stops, everybody stops and looks at the clocks. Whoever is stopped at the clock that shows the correct time...

Chorus:

Hip-hop around the clock

Hip-hop around the clock

If you're at the time you say

Hip-hop, Hip-hop, then the time on the clock.

Hip-hop around the clock

Hip-hop around the clock

Now the time is __ o'clock.

Hip-hop, Hip-hop, it's _ o'clock..

Activity Two

Fill in the blanks by asking each other the appropriate questions:-

Sheet number (1)

Ahmed	
1:35	
	arrive home
2:50	
	start homework
7:05	
	read a story
9:25	

Sheet number (2)

Ahmed	
	leave school
2:10	
	have lunch
4:00	
	watch TV
8:15	
	have dinner

Lesson Three

Our holiday

- *Objectives: -*

  By the end of the lesson, you are expected to:

  - *Describe famous places in Egypt with adjectives.*

  - *Describe a holiday.*

- *Activity type:* pair-workgroup-work

- *Time needed:* 45 minutes

Activity One

Telephone call for asking about information

You have to phone the Egyptian Tourist Company representatives (students behind them) "and ask for information you need and write them down on the task sheet.

- *Tourist*: - Hallo, is that the Egyptian Tourist Company?

- *Representative*: - Yes, can I help you?

- *Tourist*: - Excuse me, I'm a tourist and I want to visit Egypt?

- *Representative*: -You are welcome, we have a fantastic book for a week.

- *Tourist*: - Alright, what places will I visit.

- *Representative*: - Cairo, Luxor and Karnak.

- *Tourist*: - How much should I pay?

- *Representative*: - 500 dollars.

- *Tourist*: - Ok, book me a visit.

Activity Two

A tourist in Egypt

- *Look at the map of Egypt. Imagine that you were tourists. In pairs ask and answer questions like the following:*

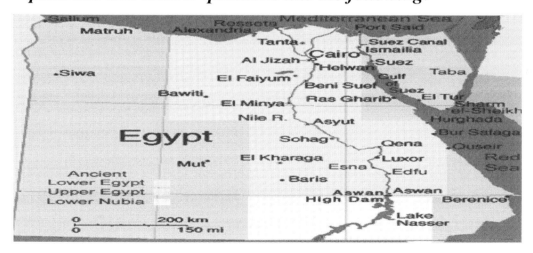

- *What will you do on Sunday morning?*

- *Where will you go?*

- *How will you go there?*

- *How long will you stay there?*

- *Where will you stay?*

- *What will you see there?*

Lesson Four

<u>This is my E-mail</u>

- **<u>*Objectives:*</u>** *-*

    By the end of the lesson, you are expected to:

    - *Invite someone for a visit.*

    - *Express plans in the future using "will".*

- **<u>*Activity type*</u>*: pairwork -groupwork*

- **<u>*Time needed*</u>*: 45 minutes*

Activity One

"Act as it is a fact"

Look at the following dialogue and set up another one with your partner

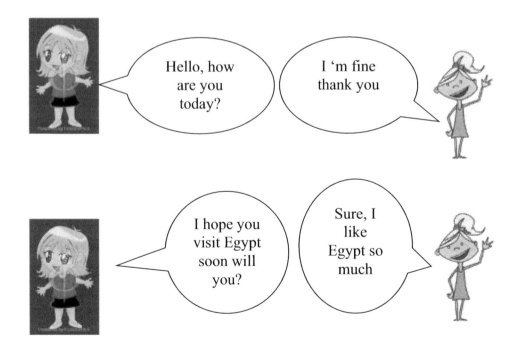

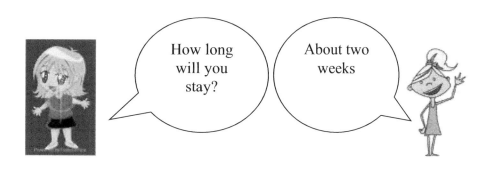

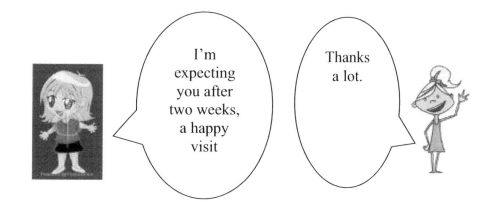

Activity Two

A lottery Winner

•*Suppose you won a million pounds in a lottery, and you have to spend the money within one hour. Write a list of things you will do, and compare them with your partner.*

Lesson Five

Don't be puzzled

- **_Objectives: -_**

  By the end of the lesson, you are expected to:

- _Practise simultaneous words (words which have the same pronunciation but different meanings._

- _Speak fluently and naturally_

- _Speak without remarkable pauses or hesitation, repetition or redundancy._

- _Use various appropriate strategic devices to enhance the clarity of the meaning such as (fillers, pauses, ellipses, etc....)._

- **_Activity type:_** _pair-workgroup-work_

- **_Time needed:_** _45 minutes_

Activity one

Rumor (Telephone)

Whispers the message you have just heard from your teacher in the next student's ear. The final student in the row says what he has heard, or draw the message on the board.

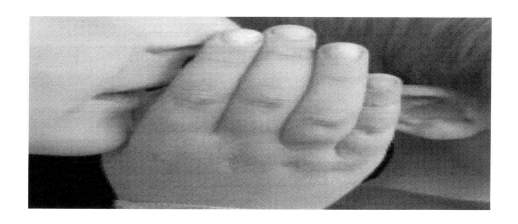

Activity Two

The One-Minute Game

▪*One member from one side speaks for one full minute about "What are your plans for the next summer holiday? The speaker has had no chance to prepare beforehand. The members of the opposing side must listen carefully and stop and disqualify the speaker the moment there is any fault or error or hesitation, etc. Then, the person who has caught the error stands up and is given a different topic.*

Unit Six

Soha's Poem

General aims:

This unit aims at helping you to:

- Tell a simple story.

- Say what was happening at specific time in the past.

- Ask and answer about what was happening in a scene.

- Describe scene in the past.

- Talk about clothes and colours.

- Predict about what is going to happen.

- Retell a story from pictures.

- Express past event that was interrupted by another action.

Lesson One

Internet magazine

- ***Objectives: -***

  By the end of the lesson, you are expected to:

  - *Tell a simple story.*

  - *Put the idea in a logical way by telling a story using first, next, then, after that and finally.*
    - ***Activity type:*** *pair-workgroup-work*
    - ***Time needed:*** *45 minutes*

Activity one

A Four-Word Story: -

- ***Tell a story in group. The first student who will start the activity writes down an English word that first comes into your mind the student sitting to his left side writes the next word which comes into his mind, but which starts with the last letter of the previous word (e.g. flower – room). Prepare to tell a short story containing words from the list. Every student in the group must say at least one sentence.***

Activity Two

Tell me what happened

- *Look at the pictures and answer the questions trying to put an end to the story.*

* The pictures of the story:

What can you see? When was the story? What did the lion say to the mouse?

Was the mouse happy? Why?

What happened to the lion?

What did it do to help the lion?

Did he succeed? How?

Think of a happy end to the story

Lesson Two

What were they doing?

- **_Objectives:_** -

    By the end of the lesson, you are expected to:

- _Talk about clothes and colours._

- _Say what was happening at specific time in the past._

- **_Activity type:_**   _pair work_
- **_Time needed:_**   _45 minutes_

Activity one

Back-to-Back

- **_Walk around the room observing other people's clothes. When the music stops, each one pairs up and you stand back-to-back. Taking turns, each of you makes statements about the other's appearances._**

Student A: I think, when I saw you, you were wearing a white jumper."

Student B: "That's not right. My jumper is blue, or

No, I was wearing a blue jumper"

Activity Two

Miming

- *Stand up in two teams facing each other in pairs. The students in the first team to mime actions using some real objects (if possible) and when your partners are sure what you mean, they shout "Stop!" They then guess the actions.*

- *It is important to say*

- *When I shouted stop.*

- *You were writing a letter.*

> *You were sleeping.*
>
> *You were washing the dishes.*
>
> *You were painting the house.*
>
> *You were eating.*

Lesson Three

A helicopter was flying in the sky

- ***Objectives: -***

    By the end of the lesson, you are expected to:

- *Use grammar structure correctly.*

- *Describe scene in the past.*

- *Ask and answer about what was happening.*

- *Activity type: pair-work*

- *Time needed: 45 minutes*

Activity one

Guess what I was doing!

- *Take a card from the top of the pile and performs your appearance and mood according to the depicted card. Your partner tries to guess the reasons behind your performance and asks you some questions.*

Crying

Were you watching a tragedy film?

Were you fighting your friends? "

Eating

Were you eating with Rasha?

Were you eating in McDonalds?

If the student guesses correctly, he or she gets a point.

Activity Two

What were they all doing?

Look at the following picture and say what they were doing when the light went out?

- *Mrs. Gamal* ....
- *Mr. Gamal* ....
- *Ahmed* ....
- *Noura* ....

Lesson Four

Retell a·story

- ***Objectives: -***

    By the end of the lesson, you are expected to:

- *Predict about what is going to happen.*

- *Retell a story from pictures.*

- *Express past event that was interrupted by another action.*

    Activity type: *pair-work*

    Time needed: *45 minutes*

Activity one

Alibi Game

Concoct a story of where you were yesterday at the time of the crime. You are then questioned separately, to see the differences between the stories.

What were you doing at 8 o'clock last night?

Where were you at 8 o'clock last night?

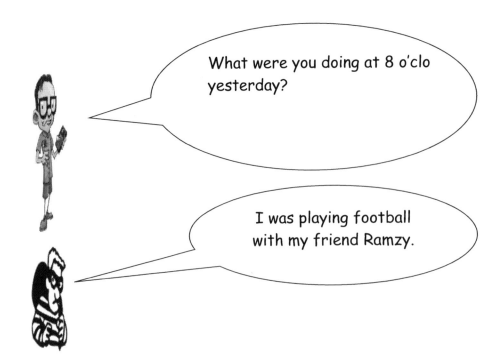

Activity Two

What is the Earliest Thing that You Remember?

Remember from your early childhood. You should write down and discuss it with your friend.

COMPLETE THE SENTENCES USING THE PAST CONTINUOUS:

1. When I was young I ....
2. My friends..
3. My parents ....
4. My grandmother ....
5. My teacher ....

My mum was always saying that if I ate too many carrots, I'd turn into one.

Lesson Five

Mother's Day

- ***Objectives: -***

  By the end of the lesson, you are expected to:

  ▪ *Use abstract vocabulary in sentences correctly.*

  ▪ *Use concrete vocabulary in sentences correctly.*

  ▪ *Speak fluently and naturally.*

  ▪ *Speak without remarkable pauses or hesitation, repetition or redundancy.*

  - ***Activity type: pair-work***
  - ***Time needed:*** *45 minutes*

Activity one

Public speaking

- ***Think for about 5 minutes to plan for a semi-impromptu and short speech to describe your kind mother.***

Activity Two
The better prize

•*Listen to the following poem about mother. Express your point of view and then try to compose your own poem about mother. You can participate with your partner.*

The Better Prize

I see you're tired when I get home.

You feel some days you're all alone.

But what you're doing is priceless, dear,

And one day you'll back–one year.

Far from now when these kids are grown,

You'll remember the days you spent at home.

Wiping noses, washing dishes,

Having tea parties, getting kisses.

Playing ball and tying shoes,

Then you'll look at me with tearful eyes,

and know you got the better prize.

Author Unknown

Printed in Great Britain
by Amazon

12292794R00047